HOW TO MAKE THE LAW OF ATTRACTION WORK FOR YOU

A Simple Guide to Creating the Reality You Want

Mike England

To Lin
You are fab go out
inspire the world with your light
and enjoy your success, happiness
& abundance

mike England

authorHOUSE®

AuthorHouse™ UK Ltd.
500 Avebury Boulevard
Central Milton Keynes, MK9 2BE
www.authorhouse.co.uk
Phone: 08001974150

First published by AuthorHouse 5/19/2009

ISBN: 978-1-4389-8166-6 (sc)

This book is printed on acid-free paper.

CONTENTS

Part One: Principles

Part Two: Techniques

Part Three: Conclusion

Part One
<u>PRINCIPLES</u>

Chapter 1

INTRODUCTION

YOU ARE HOLDING IN YOUR hands, possibly one of the most powerful books you will ever read. This book contains within its covers all the principles and techniques that you will ever need to access the awesome power of you mind and make the law of attraction work for you.

Hi, my name is Mike England, I am currently a hypnotherapist and have been working in this field since 2003. However, my interest in the vast potential of the mind that we all have has fascinated me for most of my life. This book has been produced as a result of my work and interest within this field. I have achieved success in many areas of my life, and the lives of the clients I have been working with utilizing this awesome power that we all possess. Within these pages are all the tools and keys you need to allow you to tap into your own potential. By doing so, allow the powerful law of attraction to work for you in a positive way, to bring to you all the things that you want, whether it be bringing new relationships, greater prosperity, improved health, new friends, new job, new car, in fact anything that you can think of. Absolutely anything can be attracted to you once you understand and apply the principles and techniques described in this book.

The techniques are simple and can be used by all to access the full potential of your thoughts and emotions. To literally begin attracting all the things that you want in your life.

The first section of this book describes the Law of Attraction and how it is affected by the thoughts we think, and the emotions we feel. It also contains detailed information on how beliefs play a major part in creating your reality, the reality you are experiencing right now, literally how we think things into being. Explanations are also given as to how you are attracting the things that you are getting in your life right now. Your thoughts and emotions can be changed to begin attracting the life you choose, the circumstances, and the outcomes you desire.

The second part of this book has practical techniques, which if applied faithfully, can begin to change your thoughts, emotions and beliefs so that you can begin attracting the life you choose. Outdated beliefs and thought patterns can be altered, creating new, more appropriate thought patterns which then become your new beliefs. Once this happens the law of attraction will then respond to those new beliefs and patterns of thought, creating the reality that you choose for your life.

The third part of this book is a question and answer section which addresses common areas where you may come across obstacles or challenges and possible causes and solutions for overcoming them. Explanations are given as to why, sometimes, it can appear that smaller things are easier to attract than the larger things which would create complete life changes.

So if you want to begin to create your own reality, the life that you choose, then please read on............

Chapter 2

THE LAW OF ATTRACTION

WHAT IS THE LAW OF attraction? Well basically to explain this I need to explain a little about the reality you perceive. Everything that you experience in life, your surroundings the room you are in, the book you are reading, are not really as they seem. If you could obtain a powerful enough microscope to enable you to see things on a quantum (very small microscopic) level, you would see that everything around you, the table, the chair you are sitting on, even the skin you are in, is not really solid. You would see the atoms and molecules moving or vibrating at a very fast rate. You would also notice that everything is moving or vibrating at its own particular speed. The speed of the vibration determines what you are seeing and experiencing in the physical world The Law of Attraction is basically the binding force orchestrating like for like atoms, to be attracted to each other.

The other thing that I would like you to be aware of is that your thoughts and emotions also emit an energy. You may have felt this when you walk into a room and instantly know that there is tension, or an argument has taken place, or that people are happy or excited. What is happening is that you are picking up on the dominant energy or vibrational rate of the persons within the room. Some psychics claim to be able to see this energy field and even diagnose physical disorders and illnesses within the body.

The wonderful thing to know about the law of attraction is that you can direct the Law of Attraction to work for you, so that it can attract to you all the things that you want. The process that is involved in order to do this, is that you become aware of the thoughts, feelings and beliefs that you have. You are constantly emitting signals which the law of attraction is responding to, attracting all the experiences that you are currently having and living into your life.

Your attraction power comes from the way you feel. If your thoughts and emotions are utilized in the right way you can begin emitting new signals which enables you to positively attract all the things that you want in your life.

It is very similar to the way a magnet attracts metal towards it. If you could imagine that your thoughts and emotions are the magnet, and the law of attraction is responding to those signals, this means that the law of attraction is literally attracting all the experiences in your life that match the dominant thoughts feelings and beliefs that you have. The exciting thing about all of this is that you have within you, at any given time, the ability to change the way you think and feel about any subject at all. This would then create new beliefs and patterns of thought, which in turn would attract new experiences into your life, that match the new beliefs and thought patterns. The Law of Attraction does not understand right or wrong, what you want or do not want, it just responds to the signals you emit. However if you are constantly focused on not having enough money, or not having good health, or not having that new relationship, not liking the body shape you have, then those are the signals you will emit, so you will attract those very experiences into your life. If instead you were to focus on the solution or the improvement of whatever it is that you want, you will then begin to notice gradual change until the new beliefs are established and dominant within you. Then you will begin to attract the new experiences and things that you have asked for.

If you could imagine life like one large mirror, and as you look out into the world, and the experiences of your life (the mirror), everything you experience and perceive is a complete and total reflection of everything that you have been thinking and feeling. This is a difficult concept for most people to understand, but once it is understood, a wonderful empowerment can occur, because you can come to the full realisation that you can actually change anything in your life, any situation, any experience, you can literally create your own reality.

By means of the exercises in this book, you can reach what I like to call a tipping point, this is a point where the new thoughts and feelings become so dominant within you that they become your new beliefs and habitual patterns of thought. It is when this happens that you get that job, receive that greater prosperity, see an improvement in your health, achieve the body weight you desire. This is because your new beliefs are now emitting new signals, and the law of attraction will now be responding to those new beliefs. The Method and time required to reach this tipping point is different for everyone, but if you apply the principles and techniques outlined within these pages faithfully, into your life the tipping point can be reached, and reached very quickly.

The Law of Attraction is like one huge gigantic wishing well, where everything you have ever wanted or wished for can happen or come to you. However in order to let the law of attraction bring those things to you, you need to be in a place of **trust belief** and **positive expectation** about the things that you want. The most crucial thing to understand is the fact of focusing on what you want **until you actually believe.** Once this happens the experience or things that you have wanted, come to you. The aim of this book is to transform outdated beliefs and patterns of thought so you achieve that point of belief with all the things you want to attract.

Chapter 3

THE THINKING AND EMOTIONAL MIND

THE FIRST STEP IN MAKING the law of attraction work for you; is to understand a bit more about your own mind. There are two commonly agreed terms when talking about different aspects of the mind. They are the conscious mind and the subconscious mind. I will give a brief description of both aspects below:-

Conscious Mind (Thinking Mind)

This is the part of your mind that is analytical / critical, it is the part of you that allows you to focus and concentrate on whatever task you are performing at the time, which requires your attention. It is the part of you that you utilise when you are studying or learning a new task. This part of your mind can be very critical. I refer to this part of the mind as the thinking mind and will refer to it as such for the rest of this book.

The thinking mind can hold between six and nine pieces of information at any one time. So if you begin to think about several tasks now, brushing your teeth, cooking the dinner, visiting a friend, the things to do at work and so on, when you get to between six and nine things, your mind can feel full, or confused or muddled. This is because this part of your mind can only process so much information at any one time. It is not so effective at multi tasking. That is where the subconscious mind comes in.

Subconscious Mind (Emotional Mind)

This aspect of your mind is extremely powerful; it deals with all the processes and things that the conscious mind cannot. Here is where all of your memories are stored, your habits, your beliefs, it also the point where all of your emotions are seated. The subconscious mind is also responsible for the autonomic system which deals with all the bodies' natural functions.

This part of your mind is fantastic at mult-skilling. Think about what is happening now. You are reading this book, your muscles are controlled to hold the book, you are recognizing the black shapes on white paper as letters, forming them into words, and sentences, accessing the stored memories that let you know what those words mean. Whilst all this is going on. Your blood pressure is maintained, your body temperature and breathing are perfectly regulated. Your heart beat continues, you blink and so on. So many things happen below the surface which you have no conscious awareness of. These are all the functions of the subconscious mind or as I refer to it the emotional mind, which I will continue to call it, for the rest of this book.

The Thinking And Emotional Mind

There are a lot of instances where the thinking mind and the emotional mind work in perfect harmony together: an example of this is when you think about going on holiday (thinking mind), and feel really positive and happy about going (emotional mind). When they work in harmony it is like life seems to flow easily, synchronicities happen, you would find the best deal, the places you always wanted to go at the right price everything would seem so effortless. When your emotional and thinking mind work in harmony you have created what's called positive attraction, in other words the law of attraction is responding to you in a very positive way, drawing all the things you want and are thinking and feeling about, towards you.

However, if you were to think it would be nice to go on holiday (thinking mind) and felt that there is not enough money to go (emotional mind). This is a perfect example of when the two aspects of your mind the emotional and thinking mind are not working in harmony. In other words you want something (thinking mind), and you then believe you cannot have it or achieve it (emotional mind); basically a contradiction has occurred in the two aspects of the mind. At these times you are creating what's called negative attraction, which means the law of attraction is responding to the negative signals attracting more things to be negative and feel negative about. You can begin to change your current beliefs and habitual patterns of thoughts so that you can then let the law of attraction bring everything into being that you want to experience, by understanding the law of attraction and the minds role, your life can become the life that you want.

Chapter 4
LANGUAGE AND ITS EFFECT ON YOU

MANY PEOPLE ARE TRULY NOT aware of the power of words and language and its effect on the emotions. Nearly all words and sentences create an emotional response to a greater or lesser degree. Some responses are felt greatly and others only fleetingly, however once an emotional state is activated whether it be positive or negative, it affects your point of attraction. Talking with all the people in your experience of life activates responses. Just think about when you are angry with someone and how that affects you, compared to when you are having a wonderful conversation with someone who is praising you.

Let's look at a few phrases in the examples below:

Read the statements below and notice how you feel as you read them.

You are stupid
Money does not grow on trees you know.
You will never do it
Life is supposed to be hard
You have to work hard to succeed
You won't lose weight if you don't try
You will never do any good
You are clumsy
You're always ill
You are absent minded

These are just a few, but notice how you felt as you read them. If you are like most people, you probably experienced a negative emotion to varying degrees, maybe a feeling of having to increase effort or a feeling of uphill struggle, or not wanting to bother even try.

Now reads the words below about the same subject.

You are a wonderful person with a great capacity to learn and understand, and that stupid thing you did was just one of those things, not worth even thinking or worrying about.

There is nothing you cannot achieve, the potential to earn lots of money is all out there waiting in the experiences of life, just notice and be aware for opportunities and possibilities for money to flow endlessly to you and they will come.

You can do anything if your focus is in the right direction, you have this wonderful brain that enjoys learning and understanding new things, so as you focus on this notice how easy things are for you.

Life is supposed to be fun for you, if it does not feel like fun do not do it.

Success is so easily attainable for you, because success is about doing things and achieving things that feel wonderful.

If you begin to focus on your emotional mind beginning to help you, it can direct you and motivate you to the foods and movement of the body that can allow your body to become the size and shape that you are comfortable with.

If you do things that are fun you will always succeed

Your body reflects what you feel so as you feel good, your body begins to reflect that too.

You have a fantastic memory with a powerful ability to recall anything you choose at any time.

Notice the same subjects have been used, but how the emotion feels different as you read the phrases, they are so much more empowering, so much freer. If you were to have conversations with people around you and the responses were similar to the phrases above in every subject, just imagine how easily your life would change, as a result of the positive emotion coming forth from the words spoken. In turn that would alter your beliefs and point of attraction in a more positive way.

The point I am trying to make is that if most people are affected by language you can begin to think and most importantly feel differently about the things people say and do, and direct the conversations in a more positive way. Eventually you would not engage in conversations which evoke a negative response because your point of attraction will have changed and those experiences will not come into your life. Instead, you would attract stimulating exhilarating, interesting, conversations that always let you feel good.

In section two of the book I will cover language and words again in the section called affirmation techniques whereby, you can learn how to word things in a different way a positive way so that your emotional mind can begin working for you in a much more effective way, I will teach you techniques to counteract negative conversations and comments made to you by others. However, for now, it is just enough for you to be aware of it and now you are more aware, you may find yourself being more focused when people are talking to you, noticing the emotional responses you are experiencing.

Chapter 5
CHALLENGING BELIEFS

WHAT ARE BELIEFS? WELL BELIEFS are thoughts you have been consistently thinking over a period of time. The thoughts and associated emotional responses have become so dominant within you that they have become self sustaining (or a belief). A lot of beliefs serve you extremely well and allow you to live your life in the knowledge and expectation that everything is fine. A few are listed below:-

You expect to wake up in the morning.
You expect day to follow night
You expect there to always be taxes and a government
You expect to be able to read these words
You expect your body to keep functioning in the way it does
You expect to digest food when you eat it
You expect to go to work and have your
pay cheque at the same time.

Then there are beliefs that may not serve you as well as they should, a few are detailed below:-

I have to work hard to succeed
It's so difficult to lose weight
I will never be rich
Nothing in life comes easy
I will never be able to afford that
I never attract the right relationship.

You may have some of the above beliefs or even think of more as there are lots of them. The thing for you to be aware of is that all of them at sometime have been created because you focused on a particular train of thought, situation, conversation or incident, and those thoughts have then achieved the tipping point and created the belief.

The great thing about beliefs is that they are not permanent, and are easier to change than you might think. My work as a hypnotherapist primarily involves assisting people to change outdated, inappropriate belief systems and create new patterns of thought, which in turn creates the new belief system.

If you remember what we talked about earlier, a belief creates an emotional response whether it is negative or positive, so by changing your beliefs this creates new emotional responses. You then begin to emit new signals which the law of attraction responds to, allowing you to attract all the experiences and things that you want in your life for your life.

I would like you to look at the table below it details some of the most commonly held beliefs that many people have, regarding different areas of life. The first is the current commonly held belief; The second is the new more appropriate belief. What I would like you to do is to notice the way you feel, when you read the statements listed under current beliefs. Then compare the way you feel when you read the statement under new beliefs.

The Body

CURRENT BELIEF	NEW BELIEF
It's so hard to lose weight, I am so fat	It's wonderful to know I can trust my body to attract me to the right foods, allowing me to become the size and shape that I choose.
I feel ugly and unattractive	I feel so good in my own skin, knowing I am unique and there is only one of me, I feel so good about the way I look.
I look and feel so frail and old	If my thoughts dictate the way I feel and my body responds to this I can feel wonderfully energised and invigorated just like I did in my youth, I look forward to this happening.
I am too thin	My body is becoming the size and shape that makes me feel comfortable and happy.
It's hard to stop smoking	I feel healthy and happy now I am free from that little white stick.

I feel sick / bad	My body is so good at achieving harmony and balance
This condition will never go	My body created this problem that I have, and also has the solution to the problem; I am choosing to trust in my body to sort this out.

CAREER / WORK

I hate going to work	I could begin looking for a new job / career that is more satisfying and fun. It could be exciting to look for new opportunities.
I'm scared to try something new	It is exciting to think about new challenges and experiences, I remember how I felt when I first did this job it was exciting and in just a short time it felt really comfortable.
I need to keep this job for security for me and my family	There are many career paths that can lead to security. I could easily make the decision to learn something new no decisions have to be made now but it would be good to look at new options and avenues.
I really don't get on with those people at work.	Perhaps they are not feeling good themselves, perhaps I really do not understand what they are going through and perhaps it is nothing to do with me that we do not get on.

MONEY	
I can never afford the things I want.	There is an abundance of money in the world with many opportunities everywhere to let it flow. If I put my mind to it I am sure opportunities for attracting more money could flow to me.
It's not fair they are rich and I am not	There are lots of people who have been where I am, and are financially better off, I could be one of them, there is nothing to stop me, and it's all about my focus. I think I will begin to focus more on money coming to me.
I don't deserve to be successful	I am a unique person with unique talents and abilities and deserve good things to happen and come to me.
GENERAL	
Things never go right for me	Some things go wrong but I always know how to put them right
I feel guilty	I have freedom to think what I choose
I'm not very confident.	I love talking to people and meeting new people I am so confident.
I am scared of flying	Its fun to think about getting on a plane and flying anywhere in the world

RELATIONSHIPS	
I always attract the same type of man / woman	There are all sorts of people out there and its going to be so nice to explore the variety of people who come into my life. Some will be compatible other not so compatible but I will know who is perfect for me.
My partners always leave me.	It's good to know that my life is moving forward in the right direction moving toward the perfect partner for me. I feel secure thinking about this and that special person coming into my life.
My partner always criticizes me.	That's ok I do not have to react to what they say, I feel what I feel and they feel what they feel, and I choose to let this go, its not important.

There are many more beliefs I could list on numerous subjects and even more on the subjects above. The above are just examples of some beliefs common to everyone. Did you notice how you felt as you read them. A lot of people notice that the current belief creates a negative emotional response, and the new beliefs create a positive emotional response. So you have probably guessed it is really important to understand about beliefs in order to change your point of attraction and allow the law of attraction to work for you in bringing everything that you want.

I would like you to choose a particular area of your life, whether it is work, money, relationships, more friends, that new car, or even a car parking space at the shopping centre. I would like you to obtain a pen and piece of paper and write at the top current beliefs. Then I would like you to list your current beliefs regarding the subject you have chosen, and what you would like the new belief to be

Two examples are given below:-

Current belief

Shopping centre example

The shopping centre is really busy today; it will be difficult to find a space.

It always seems like everyone else has the parking spaces and there is never one for me.

New belief

It's really good to know that a parking space will be waiting for me when I arrive.

Current Belief

New car example

I cannot afford that car, I barely have enough money to pay the bills
I will never be able to afford that its out of my reach
I feel really disappointed about it.

New Belief

There are many things I own know which I believed I could not afford.

I found a way to bring more money to attract those things, I could do it for this.

Its so nice to think about having that new car, I can imagine the feel of the steering wheel, the seats, driving the car down the road with everyone looking in admiration, this feels good. I know if I continue to focus in this way opportunities can arrive into my life that will allow that car to come to me. Yes this feels really good I am going to enjoy thinking more about this.

Now keep this page of the current and new beliefs that you have written regarding the subject you have chosen. We will be using this in the second part of the book. Now as we close this chapter, you are aware of all the principles to enable you to apply the techniques and begin attracting into your life all the things that you want. So please read on........

Part Two
TECHNIQUES

Chapter 6
BEFORE WE BEGIN

DETAILED IN THIS SECTION OF the book are extremely powerful techniques to begin using the awesome power of your mind. Do not be fooled by the simplicity of the techniques. They can have a major impact upon you and your life. Once you apply them and begin to change your beliefs (dominant thought patterns), you will then be able to use the power of the law of attraction to bring to you the things that you want.

The techniques described can be used as many times as you wish on many varying subjects in your life. As you begin to utilise them you will begin training your mind and thought processes allowing your mind to begin working for you in a much more positive way. We have discussed how the law of attraction responds to the signals you emit and the signals you emit are created from the emotional responses experienced, regarding the beliefs and patterns of thoughts you have about whatever subject it is that you are focused upon.

The chapters detailing the techniques will be separated into three sections. The first section details the best situations to apply the particular technique being discussed. The second part details how to use the technique. The third part describes a summary of the technique and what you are likely to experience.

Always remember that each and every person on the planet is unique and individual and as a result of this each, person who carries out the technique will have different experiences and results with varying degrees of success. There is no right or wrong in any of this but if you approach each technique with an open mind and really want what you are focused upon, that is all that is required to achieve success.

Some of you will experience immediate results with the techniques described herein, others may need to perform them several times before results are noticeable. In either case if you are faithful in your application of the techniques results will be obtained.

When teaching these techniques I always teach people to utilise the techniques with small things first so that they can actually begin to see the results. Once results are forthcoming it reinforces your belief in the techniques and your own ability to attract anything you want. Examples of some small things could be manifesting a car parking space, or a coloured feather or favourite film to be available for you to watch, or even a favourite song to be playing on the radio, anything really where there are no major belief systems surrounding the subject. I will just tell you a story about when I first began manifesting and attracting things into my life:-

When I first started I manifested a black feather with a white stripe. That was not enough for me so I then proceeded to manifest a pink feather and a fluorescent green feather, then a scarlet feather they all came and very quickly. It was when

I got to the peacock feather I began to understand more about belief systems. I basically set about manifesting a peacock feather and stated that this is not likely to come at this time of year because it is the winter. Four weeks went by and it still had not come (that is a long time for something to manifest in my life). Then I began to go over the techniques which I describe later on, and realized that I had created a negative belief when I stated its winter so not likely to come at this time of year. I worked on the belief and within 7 days I went to a friends house, she wanted a hypnotherapy session. After the session I looked on the window sill and what was sitting in a vase **A Peacock Feather,** I laughed and my friend asked me why, I told her, and she said you can have that if you want it. I said "no it's enough that I have seen it". Well, that taught me a valuable lesson about how beliefs affect our point of attraction. Just to complete the story for about two months after that everywhere I went there were peacock feathers, it was amazing, as if the law of attraction was saying now you believe we will keep bringing them. I love knowing that everything in my life is created by me and my thoughts and you will too as you begin experiencing the awesome power of your mind, and its fantastic ability to affect the law of attraction to bring to you whatever you want.

The first thing that is required as a pre requisite to any of the techniques outlined in this section of the book is relaxation. You are continually communicating with your emotional mind all through the day. To actually begin affecting your emotional mind and begin changing beliefs and patterns of thoughts it requires that you allow the thinking mind to go into abeyance for awhile. It is very much like when you are sunbathing on a beach daydreaming and just enjoying the fantasy, you do not care whether the fantasy is real or not you are just enjoying the experience, It is that state of mind I want you to achieve. So let us begin to show you a great technique for achieving the level of relaxation required.

Chapter 7

RELAXATION A PRE REQUISITE

THE PURPOSE OF RELAXATION PRIOR to using the techniques is to increase the effectiveness of the techniques. If you remember earlier, I stated that the thinking mind and emotional mind sometimes have contradictory beliefs and the thinking mind can be very analytical and critical of new ideas. When a relaxed state of mind and body is created, the thinking mind can go into a subdued state you are still aware of everything, but it can reduce the amount of critical and sometimes even sceptical thoughts from taking hold. This allows you to communicate more fully with the emotional mind to create the changes that you want, attracting the things that you want.

How is this state of mind achieved? The fantastic thing is that you have done it many times before in your life. For example when you have ever read a book, or watched a film and are totally engrossed in the film or book, You do not sit there thinking that's not real, that's impossible, this is ridiculous, no, all that you do is watch the film or read the book and enjoy the experience. These are situations where the thinking mind has gone into abeyance.

An exercise for achieving a state of relaxation for the mind and body is detailed below:-

I would like you to turn the phones off and ensure that you will not be disturbed for at least 20 - 30 minutes. Then sit or lie in a comfortable position, ensure you have loose clothing on, and that the room is warm.

Now as you sit or lie ensure your legs and arms are not crossed but flat on the chair or bed.

Now close your eyes and begin to focus on your breathing, do not change it in anyway, just focus on the air moving in through your nose, notice it as it moves through your air ways and into the various passageways of the lungs. As you expel the air from your mouth just imagine the old oxygen leaving the body like a dark mist, or just a feeling of releasing the tension and cares of the day. Nothing is more important than you focus on your breathing, nothing matters. Just do this in a very casual natural way, allowing your breathing to find its own rhythm. After about 10 breaths in and out, you may notice your breathing becoming slower and longer, this is perfectly natural just allow your body to do whatever it chooses, just continue to focus on each breath. Remember, there is no right or wrong way, you are not trying to achieve anything, you are just noticing your breath as it moves in and out of your body in a gentle rhythm.

After about ten breaths begin to say to yourself silently and mentally Peace, peace, peace, allow the words to be slow and methodical, wonderfully effortless as the words flow through your mind. Eventually you may notice that as you mentally say the word peace it flows out each time you breathe out. Notice your body responding to your rhythmic breathing and the calm tranquil feeling within your body.

At this point you may experience a sense of clarity, or calmness or lightness or heaviness of the body. You may experience nothing very much different from what you usually feel but know that what you do experience is just right for you. Whilst you continue to do this over several minutes, you may notice your thoughts beginning to drift into your imagination, or your memories, and that is perfectly ok, allow your thoughts to drift where they will. Do not try and hold on to them just allow them to flow in and out of your experience.

As you achieve this wonderful tranquil feeling state, you can continue to experience this state for as long as you choose usually about 20 to 30 minutes is sufficient.

When you are ready to bring yourself out of this calm peaceful state it is always a good idea to count yourself out of it gradually allowing your body to return to its normal waking state. Sometimes just opening your eyes, which you can do at anytime, does not always give the body the time it needs to awaken, very much like that feeling you can experience when an alarm goes off after a nights sleep. The best way is to just state inside yourself I will awaken as I count up from 1 to 5, each number I count, I am becoming more and more alert and on 5 I will open my eyes to a fully awakened state.

Then just count up from 1 to 5 and open your eyes.

I would like you to practice this exercise once a day over a period of five or seven days, so that your mind and body can learn how to achieve the required state of relaxation quickly and easily. You will then be ready to actually begin applying the techniques in the forthcoming chapters. When you become adept at applying the techniques no relaxation is required, but it is always good at the start.

CHAPTER 8
THE AGREEMENT TECHNIQUE

When to use this technique:-

THIS TECHNIQUE IS BASICALLY WHAT it implies and that is to get the emotional mind to agree to the new belief / patterns of thoughts around the object of your attention. Which in turn creates a new emotional response allowing the law of attraction to bring to you the things that you want.

This technique requires that you be in a relaxed state, so that you can disassociate from the beliefs that you have. It is good to use this technique if there are between one and five inappropriate beliefs regarding the subject of your attention, in other words what you want to attract.

I will detail below an example of how the technique can be used and applied. I will first describe what is wanted, then the current beliefs surrounding it. Then I will detail the new beliefs, and finally the application of the technique to create the new beliefs, thereby, attracting what you want into your experience.

If for any reason you are having difficulty identifying your current beliefs regarding what you want to attract, just think about what you do want and notice how you feel. If you feel a negative emotional response, then there are beliefs that are preventing you from attracting what you want, so begin to focus on those beliefs and list them.

The example below is just an example but there is no reason why you could not use this technique to attract a new car, improved health, in fact anything you wish. Just remember it works better when there are between 1 and 5 beliefs surrounding the things that you want.

Example

Write on a piece of paper

What is it that I want to attract or experience?

I want a brand new car

What are my current beliefs regarding this?

I cannot afford that new car.
I feel so upset that I never have enough money for anything that I want.
I will just have to buy a second hand car.
It seems I always have to make do.

What new beliefs do I want to create regarding a new car?

It's great to know that I can attract anything into my life. Now I have made the decision to have that brand new car, I have begun the process of attracting it I can just sit back relax and let it come to me.

Application of Technique:-

Now you have clarified your beliefs regarding what you want to attract, you can begin applying the Agreement Technique.

What I would like you to do first is to read the piece of paper you have, so the current and new beliefs are fresh in your mind.

The next step is to achieve a relaxed state of mind and body using the relaxation technique described in chapter 7 of this book.

Now you are relaxed I would like you to begin to think about the emotional mind and thinking mind as separate parts of yourself, almost like two different people. If it helps you could imagine a mirror image of yourself inside your mind that represents your emotional mind. Then invite your emotional mind into the experience that you are having.

The emotional part of yourself is like a foreman in a factory ensuring everything functions as it should and all the different parts of the mind and body work as you want them to work. It is like one great big team working together in harmony.

Now you have invited the emotional mind into your experience I would like you to have a conversation with your emotional mind about the thing or experience you want to attract. The conversation could go something like the one below:-

You

Thanks for coming, I had to meet you because I want to attract a brand new car into my experience. However, it seems that the beliefs that I have developed over the years are preventing me from achieving that.

I would like you to help me to create new beliefs and patterns of thoughts so that the law of attraction can respond to them attracting to me the brand new car that I want.

Emotional Mind Response

This can vary from person to person, however usually it requires you negotiating with your emotional mind to come to some form of agreement that both of you can agree with. It may go something like below:-

I did not realise that was what you were trying to do, I was sending you those negative emotions to let you know that you were off track. In other words I thought you wanted the beliefs you had and that they were serving you well. They have served you well most of your life.

You

Yes, they have, however, they are inappropriate now. I am older and wiser and understand so much more about what I want from life. This brand new car, I really really want, and I would like you to help me get it. Can you do that please?

Emotional Mind

I can yes, but I am not sure what you want me to do. What would help you to get it?

You

A new belief would allow the law of attraction to respond to me in a different way bringing the new car into my experience. Instead of those old beliefs I would like to believe something different and have a really positive feeling, a feeling of positive expectation that what I have asked for is on its way to me already, so that when I say and use these words:-

It's great to know that I can attract anything into my life, Now I have made the decision to have that brand new car, I have begun the process of attracting it, I can just sit back relax and let it come to me.

I can really believe and trust in it. This will then allow the law of attraction to bring the new car to me. I know you can do this for me; you have already created so many beliefs that serve me well.

Emotional Mind

Yes I can do that when do you want me to start?

You

Right now please, and thank you so much,

Now it is strange to explain because everyone feels something different but at this point you may feel a sense of satisfaction, or a really positive calm feeling. Whatever you experience, it is just your emotional mind letting you know that it has agreed to do what you have asked.

The final part of the technique is to continue to think about the new belief within you over and over, imagine driving that new car and how it feels, hearing your emotional mind stating the belief over and over, allowing you to experience more and more positive emotion as it flows through your body. Do this for as long as you choose, but long enough so that the positive emotion is firmly embedded within you.

It is just a matter of thanking your emotional mind and let it go to do the job you have asked it to do. Then you can count yourself up and out of this relaxed state and go on with your day.

The other thing to add is that it is a good idea to think about the new belief many times through the day and just before you go to bed at night continually reinforcing it, allowing the law of attraction to bring it to you more quickly. The other thing about this technique is to continue to go into the relaxed state described earlier a few times a week and continue to meet with your emotional mind, reinforcing the conversation until what you have asked for has manifested. The conversation could be something along along the lines of below:-

You

I just thought I would say I have had a wonderful week. I have been more and more positive about the car coming to me. I just feel really good about it.

Emotional Mind

Thank you I am glad I am doing a good job for you

It's really just a reinforcement of what has been done, it does not have to be long and drawn out, it is just more of an acknowledgement of the work you have already done.

Summary

To summarize, this technique is about asking your emotional mind to agree to a new set of beliefs this then allows the law of attraction to respond to you in a different way bringing whatever it is you have asked for into your life.

It does not matter whether the conversation you have with your emotional mind is the same as above or along similar lines. The most important thing is that it agrees to the changes to a point where you can feel the satisfaction of the agreement that has been made.

You then envision yourself with the things or experiences you want to attract in your life and continue to state, and most importantly feel the positive emotion as you state the new beliefs many times throughout your day.

The conversations after this are just to reinforce the belief further, which expedite the changes allowing things to come to you more quickly.

Chapter 9
THE MOVIE STRIP TECHNIQUE

When to use this technique:-

THIS TECHNIQUE IS EXTREMELY GOOD if you are visual and imaginative. It is best to use this technique if there are many beliefs surrounding the thing that you are wanting to attract.

This technique requires that you be in a relaxed state so that you can utilise your imagination to begin changing the outdated beliefs you have regarding the things you want to attract and begin creating new ones. It is good to use this technique if there are lots of inappropriate beliefs regarding the subject of your attention in other words what you want to attract.

I will detail below an example of how the technique can be used and applied. I will first describe what is wanted, then the current beliefs surrounding it. Then I will detail the new beliefs, and finally the application of the technique, to create the new beliefs, thereby, attracting what you want into your experience.

If for any reason you are having difficulty identifying your current beliefs regarding what you want to attract, just think about what you do want and notice how you feel. If you feel a negative emotional response, then there are beliefs that are preventing you from attracting what you want, so begin to focus on those beliefs and list them.

The example below is just an example but there is no reason why you could not use this technique to attract a new car, improved health, in fact anything you wish. Just remember it works better when there are more than 5 beliefs surrounding the things that you want.

Example

Write on a piece of paper

What is it that I want to attract or experience?

I want to attract a loving relationship.

What are my current beliefs regarding this?

I always seem to attract the wrong type of man / woman.
I don't deserve to meet someone nice.
The people I do meet always seem to criticize me and put me down.
Everyone else seems to have nice partners.
Why can't I meet someone nice?
I am really envious of their relationship.

As you can see there can be a lot of beliefs regarding relationships. Just list all the beliefs that you have regarding relationships.

What new beliefs do I want to attract in a loving relationship?

I want to attract a partner who is kind and loving, a person who wants to spend time with me. A person who wants to experience a loving harmonious relationship with me. I am deserving of this and believe that this person is being attracted to me right now.

Application of the Technique:-

Now you have clarified your beliefs regarding the thing that you want to attract you can begin applying the movie strip technique.

What I would like you to do first is to read the piece of paper you have so the current and new beliefs are fresh in your mind.

The next step is to achieve a relaxed state of mind and body, using the relaxation technique described earlier.

Now you are in this relaxed state, I would like you to begin to imagine that you are in a movie theatre. You are the only one in this theatre it is empty apart from you. As you look in front of you there are large curtains drawn across the movie screen. In a few moments the curtains will open and the movie will begin.

First just ponder what it is you want to attract, (the loving relationship), and begin to focus on the current beliefs you have regarding this. As you do this the curtains draw open and the movie begins. First of all you see the credits, they state: written by (your name), Produced by (your name) and then the movie begins. The movie is specific to your life and in particular your life regarding relationships. Begin to see scenes of all the relationships you have ever had. Partners, friends you have known and do know, family members in fact any person you have ever known in your life.

Notice all the conversations, the situations, the way you felt during them in fact everything. They may stretch back throughout all the years of your life into childhood. That is ok, take as long as you need to notice all of these different and varying situations, conversations, feelings and emotions you have experienced with all the different people you have ever known.

Now bring the movie to the present day. I would like you to notice right in front of you is the movies strip tape that is running that has recorded your entire life. As you notice this begin to rewind the tape back, slowly at first. When it gets to an incident where you experienced a negative experience or emotion regarding a relationship; in particular situations regarding partners you have had that have not been what you wanted, or situations where you experienced loneliness as a result of having no partner at all, stop the tape. I would like you to imagine a pair of scissors beside you and cut that piece of the tape out and throw it in the bin beside you. Notice the picture of that particular situation instantly vanish from the screen.

I would like you to continue this with every relationship where you have experienced a negative emotional response, every instance you have been lonely or sad about not having a relationship. Take your time here to do a really thorough job. If you like you can cut out a few situations each day, if there are lots, otherwise you can do them all in one session.

Once you have done this I would like you then to light a match and put the lighted match in the bin with all those old bits of tape (old beliefs) that you no longer feel are appropriate in your life. Burn them and watch them burn and feel good about them burning. Notice a strong wind begins to pick up the remaining ashes and carry them away.

What I would like you to do then is obtain a new strip of film and place it into the machine. As you do this look at the machine you will notice a record button. I want you to press it.

Now I would like you to begin to create a new movie of the life you would like, Notice the relationship that you have in your life, the conversations you have, the things you do together, the intimate words spoken and times spent together. It is like the most romantic loving film you have ever seen. Notice the emotions you are feeling as you watch this film. It may seem as though it takes on a life of its own, one that is wonderful, free and loving. Notice too that you are the star of this film living this wonderful life. Notice not just the partner and loving relationship you have there, but also the relationship with friends, family, work colleagues in fact anyone you come into contact with. It may seem that your life is just flowing wonderfully. You are so confident, happy and filled with positive emotion.

Then at a time when you are really experiencing the positive emotion within you, STEP INTO the movie and become that other you in the movie. Feel what you are feeling, see through your own eyes, be aware of being in your own body, be aware of the thoughts and beliefs you have, and the wonderful conversations you are having. Be aware of the wonderful loving relationship you have with your partner, the one who has been attracted into your life. Notice how good life is, how happy and confident you are. Spend 5 or 10 minutes doing this really being aware of the positive emotion flowing through your entire body. Then at a time of your choosing, *bring yourself out of this relaxed state by counting up from 1 to 5. As you do this bring all those wonderful positive emotions out with you.*

You can break this exercise up so that you can use the first part over a few days if you wish. Continue to cut the strips of film placing them in the bin and burning them, each time feeling freer and freer. When you have done this just bring yourself out of that state till the next time and then when you have finally cut all the strips away (inappropriate beliefs) you can then go onto the second part of creating a new movie. If you prefer you can do it all at once in one session, it is entirely up to you.

Once the new tape (beliefs) have been created it is a good idea, to repeat the last part of the exercise where you are experiencing the new movie and the new life and the new experiences until you feel that positive emotion. Then step into it and really feel what it feels like to live that life.

I would recommend that you continue this 3 or 4 times a week, until what you have asked for has been brought to you, in other words until that wonderful relationship as manifested in your life.

Summary

To summarize, this technique is very good if you are visual. It allows you to change old patterns of thoughts (beliefs) creating new ones the law of attraction can respond to. This will change the old patterns of thought, (the old movie strip with all the negative emotions), into new patterns of thought, (the new movie strip with positive emotions). This is a very effective and powerful technique for getting what you want very quickly, and dealing with a lot of beliefs all at once.

What I would also suggest is that throughout your day when you have a few moments to focus, maybe lunch time, or prior to bedtime, or when you first wake up, in fact anytime of your choosing, just ponder the new wonderful loving relationship that is being attracted to you right now. Notice how wonderful it feels. This will allow you to experience even quicker results.

Chapter 10
THE GENIE TECHNIQUE

When to use this technique:-

THIS TECHNIQUE IS EXTREMELY GOOD if the beliefs you have regarding the subject or experience you are attracting are not all that powerful, or you want to remain within you existing belief systems. An example of this would be attracting a phone call, a parking space at the supermarket, or to meet up with a particular friend, attract a small amount of money and so on. In fact any situation where you do not need to change a powerful belief system. You could use this even to stop smoking, or create a change in your eating habits to reduce your bodily weight; there are many instances where this can be used. However, if the beliefs you have about attracting large amounts of money, a successful career, the perfect relationship, the perfect health etc. are not all that powerful, or are relatively new beliefs then this technique will also work for that too.

It is best to use this technique once you have used one or two of the other techniques in this book. Once you have achieved success in some areas of your life, your belief in the power of your mind and its ability to influence the law of attraction to bring to you the things that you want, can then allow this technique to work much more powerfully for you. As with all the techniques in this book it does stand alone and can be used regardless.

This technique requires that you be in a relaxed state so that you can utilise the power of your imagination much more effectively. I will detail below an example of how the technique can be used and applied:-

Example

Write on a piece of paper

What is it that I want to attract or experience?

I will use two examples for this technique.

I want to attract more money (or state a specific amount one thousand pounds etc)

I want to lose weight

What is really important about this technique is that it works within your current belief system, creating a gradual change in your beliefs. To actually change a belief more quickly one of the other techniques may be more suitable at this time. However when you are achieving success with this technique your belief system will become stronger allowing you to use this technique in almost any circumstance (it's actually my favourite technique as its simplicity is so powerful and effective at creating change).

Current Beliefs

I know more money can come to me it has before, a thousand pounds is not a lot of money to attract it should be easy to get that.

I know I can lose weight, I see other people who have done it, and they seem to do it easily; I could find a way that is right for me.

If however, what you want is outside your current belief system for example one hundred thousand pounds or one million pounds, this technique may not be so effective.

So work with an amount of money that is believable to you. When my parents first used this technique, the washing machine, dryer and fridge all broke in one week, so my mother used this technique asking for six hundred pounds to come to her, which was believable for her. In the first week, she won some money on the lottery. In the second week my parents went on holiday to the Isle of Wight where she proceeded to win, playing bingo not once, but twice, and guess what she won in total just under six hundred pounds. Remember when using this technique remain within your current belief system. Do not focus on the how, just the amount of money you have specified.

New Beliefs

Not required for this, as this does not contradict an existing belief system within you. Gradual use of this technique will allow you to come to a place of trust and belief in the technique, allowing it to practically work under any circumstances in any conditions to attract anything.

Application of the Technique:-

The next step is to achieve a relaxed state of mind and body, using the relaxation technique described earlier.

Begin to imagine that there is a small pyramid in front of you. Notice its colour, its shape, touch it, notice the texture and temperature of the pyramid.

Notice a feeling of anticipation, maybe even excitement for what is about to happen.

Slowly begin to picture a golden mist beginning to rise from the apex (top most point) of this pyramid. It becomes brighter and clearer, the more the golden mist rises out of the top.

It then begins to form an image, this image is different for everyone, some see it as a person, others as a formless mist with a face, and some even describe seeing animals. I always notice an Arab man dressed in all the clothes ascribed, like the traditional genie in the lamp. Whatever you experience will be right for you, and dependent very much on your beliefs and culture. The important thing to recognise is that this genie can bring to you anything that you desire.

Here a booming voice state "yes master how can I serve you"

You then state your request (within your current belief system of course)

It could be something like below:-

"I want to attract one thousand pounds into my experience within 30 days, easily and effortlessly in a way that is harmonious and comfortable to me."

I want to have control over the food I eat, allowing me to become and maintain the body size and shape that I am happy with. I want to notice this change within the next month in a way that is effortless, comfortable and harmonious for me.

Always specify a time limit that is reasonable (within your current beliefs), and always make the closing statement "in a way that is effortless, comfortable and harmonious for me" You would not want to attract the money through an insurance claim due to an accident you may have, or because your boss asks you to work an extra 30hrs per week. In the example of weight control, you would not want to lose weight by being ill etc. So always make that final statement and whatever you ask for will come in an effortless and comfortable way.

Now just imagine the genie bow before you stating the words "it will be done"

Then notice the genie shrink back into the pyramid.

Only ask for one thing at each session, and do not ask for anything else until the first thing has manifested. Eventually with experience of this technique you can ask for many things at the same time. I have found this technique when first used, is better if you ask for one thing at a time.

Now count up from 1 to 5 to bring yourself out of the relaxed state you are in.

Summary

The genie technique is a good one as it actually remains within your current system of belief. This creates very gradual changes, therefore making it easier for you to attract the smaller things. This in turn allows an even bigger belief in the power of your mind to attract all the things that you want. Eventually your belief in this technique will be so strong you will be able to use it for almost anything you want to attract into your life.

Just one more thing it is a good idea that whenever you think about what you have asked for throughout your day, or remember your experience of this technique, to actually make the statement,

Below:-

"Its good to know it's all taken care of and the money is coming to me".

"It's good to know that everything is fine and I am beginning to notice the changes in the way I feel about food, and that my eating habits are beginning to change right now."

Obviously relating the statement to whatever request you have made.

This statement just increases the belief even further allowing what you have asked for to come so much more quickly. It is like a reminder to the genie (who is really your emotional mind), to continue attracting to you what you have asked for.

Chapter 11
THE GRATITUDE TECHNIQUE

When to use this Technique:-

THIS TECHNIQUE IS QUITE A good technique for working with, when you have lots of beliefs. I have used this technique a lot with clients when they have had a physical illness or medical diagnosis. It seems to work really well in these types of situations, an example of some of these, would be skin disorders, irritable bowel syndrome, allergic reactions, hay fever, asthma, celiac and so on.

I personally believe that any medical condition can be reversed if the power of the mind is used correctly to bring about a change in the beliefs, which the law of attraction can then respond to.

This technique does stand alone and can be used for anything you would like to attract whether it is more money, greater success, that holiday and so on.

This technique requires that you be in a relaxed state. It is good to use this technique if there are more than 5 beliefs regarding the subject of your attention (what you want to attract).

I will detail below an example of how the technique can be used and applied. I will first describe what is wanted, then the current beliefs surrounding it. Then I will detail the new beliefs, and finally the application of the technique to create the new beliefs, thereby, attracting what you want into your experience.

If for any reason you are having difficulty identifying your current beliefs regarding what you want to attract, just think about what you do want and notice how you feel. If you feel a negative emotional response, then there are beliefs that are preventing you from attracting what you want, so begin to focus on those beliefs and list them.

The example below is just an example but there is no reason why you could not use this technique to attract a new car, improved health in fact anything you wish. Just remember it works better when there are between a lot of beliefs surrounding the things that you want.

Example - Psoriasis / skin disorder

Write on a piece of paper

What is it that I want to attract or experience?

I want to have beautiful smooth clear skin.

What are my current beliefs regarding this?

I have had this most of my life, its never going to go.
Even the medication from the health professionals is not strong
enough to get rid of it.
It gets a lot worse when I am under stress.
I feel so unhappy no one seems to be able to help me
I am stuck with this for the rest of my life
I hate having to cover up on a beautiful summer's day
I am so self conscious of my skin

There are probably many more that could be written above; I have just described a few of the possible beliefs that some people may have who are suffering from this condition.

What new beliefs do I want to create regarding this condition?

It is going to be great to wake up one morning and notice how wonderfully smooth and clear my skin is. I have already set things in motion, and that will allow me to notice a considerable improvement in my skin within a matter of a few short days or weeks. I feel Great.

Application of Technique:-

Now you have clarified your beliefs regarding the thing that you want to attract you can begin applying the Gratitude Technique.

What I would like you to do first is to read the piece of paper you have so that the current and new beliefs are fresh in your mind.

The next step is to achieve a relaxed state of mind and body, using the relaxation technique described in the last chapter.

Now you are relaxed I would like you to begin to think about what you want to attract. "I want to have beautiful smooth clear skin"

Now become aware of your current beliefs surrounding what you want...

In the example given above that would be:

I have had this most my life, its never going to go.
Even the medication from the health professionals is not strong enough to get rid of it.
It gets a lot worse when I am under stress.
I feel so unhappy no one seems to be able to help me
I am stuck with this the rest of my life
I hate having to cover up on a beautiful summer's day
I am so self conscious of my skin

What I would like you to do is to take the first belief.

In your mind, your own thoughts I would like you to state the first current belief in your list.

I have had this most of my life, its never going to go away, (notice the emotional response you have).

Then begin saying to yourself .

Thank you so much for getting rid of this condition, I am so grateful, and so happy that you have done this for me. (continue to do this until you begin to feel a positive feeling no matter how slight)

Then take the next belief and do the same again

So inside yourself state the next belief.

Even the medication from the health professionals is not strong enough to get rid of this, (notice the emotional response you have).

Then begin saying to yourself.

Thank you so much for getting rid of this condition, I am so grateful, and so happy that you have done this for me. It is so good that I do not have to take any more medication. (Continue this until you experience a positive emotional response)

Then take the next belief and do the same again

So inside yourself state the next belief.

It gets worse when I am under stress, (until you feel the emotional response).

Then begin saying to yourself.

Thank you so much for getting rid of this condition, I am so grateful, and so happy that you have done this for me. It is so good that I can feel relaxed and calm, enjoying my beautiful smooth, clear skin. (Continue this until you experience a positive emotional response.

Continue to do this with each and every belief you have written down regarding the condition you want to change or the things you want to attract.

Once you have done this and feel the positive emotional responses within you. You can then proceed to the next part of the technique

*Once you have gone through all the beliefs relating to the things you want to attract, or condition that you want to improve, you should begin to notice a really positive emotion flowing through you. It is at this time that you begin to picture exactly what it is that you want, using the first example you would picture yourself with beautiful clear skin. (**What is really important here is that you actually picture this experience as though you are inside your own body, looking out through your own eyes**).*

Continue to do this until the positive emotion becomes really dominant.

Then at a time of your choosing, count up from 1 to 5 gradually allowing yourself to return to a normal waking state.

The technique is exactly the same whatever it is you want to attract. If you were using this technique for a better paid job, you could use something similar to the example below:

Current belief

I never seem to get a job that I am happy doing, and earn enough money to do the things that I want.

New Belief

Thank you so much for bringing this new job, I am so grateful and so happy that you have done this for me. I am so happy in my work now and am earning so much more money to do the things I want to do.

Just experience yourself feeling the satisfaction of being in a new job, and having the extra money to do the things you want to do.

It is not necessary to see yourself in a particular job, unless you know what it is that you want to do. It is just enough to have the picture and feeling of satisfaction you have on knowing there is a job that is making you happy and prosperous.

Remember the law of attraction responds to the emotional response created from the new belief. If you feel satisfied that you are in a job that is stimulating and fun, and earning more money, just capture that feeling within your imagination and that is what you will attract into your life.

So as you can see this technique can be used for any situation, or circumstance, not just for illness or medical conditions. This technique should be used everyday until what you have asked for has manifested in your life. You will notice as you use this technique that the emotional responses to the outdated beliefs you used to have will become more and more insignificant. The new beliefs and positive emotions will become stronger and stronger within you. That is a sure sign that what you have asked for is on its way to you.

Summary

What this technique actually does, is to allow your emotional mind to experience the thoughts and emotions associated with having what you want, the improved condition. If you create situations within your mind where the condition or things that you want are already there, and thank your emotional mind for the improvement, you then will begin to notice an improvement in the condition or circumstance extremely quickly.

Just a little footnote here: your emotional mind does not know the difference between your imagination and reality. Just think about this, if you were walking across a straight rope on your lounge carpet right now, you would probably find that relatively easy. Now imagine that the rope is between two cliff edges and if you stray from the rope you will fall off into the vast canyon below.

Did you notice a difference in the emotional response? Most people notice it is quite easy to walk across the rope on the lounge floor, but when faced with the prospect of walking across the SAME rope between two cliff edges, it can create anxiety, fear and all sorts of negative emotions.

If you think of the above example there is nothing different between them other than the utilisation of your imagination. Imagine what you can do when you begin to use this power to get the things that you want!

Chapter 12
THE LET IT GO TECHNIQUE

When to use the Technique

THIS TECHNIQUE IS EXTREMELY USEFUL if you have a lot of beliefs (more than 5.) It is also a very useful technique if you are quite sceptical or pessimistic. This technique does not require you to change your beliefs in the same way as the techniques described in previous chapters, or to utilise your imagination in a powerful way.

The other great thing about this technique is it can be used at anytime under any circumstances. It can be used whilst in a relaxed state and I would always recommend that it be used in this way at least twice per week. It can also be used in everyday life as you are going about your day to day business.

I will detail below an example of how the technique can be used and applied. I will first describe what is wanted, then the current beliefs surrounding it and then the process of applying the Let it Go technique.

Example

Write on a piece of paper

What is it that I want to attract or experience?

I want to own my own successful business.

What are my current beliefs regarding this?

I could never do that, I am not very intelligent.
I fail at everything I do.
I would not know where to begin.
I have lots of ideas but am scared that things will not work out.
I am not meant to succeed.
What if I do this and it fails.
What if I do not earn enough to support me and my family?

There are many beliefs that could be associated with the example described above, just list them all, and if you think of anymore, just add them to the list.

Now you have clarified your beliefs regarding the thing(s) that you want to attract you can begin applying the Let It Go Technique.

Application of the Technique

What I would like you to do first is for you to read the piece of paper you have so the current beliefs are fresh in your mind. The first time you use this technique it is best to achieve a relaxed state of mind and body, using the relaxation technique described earlier. The thing about this technique is that it requires no real effort on your part. The first thing to do is to focus on what you want to attract:-

I want to own my own successful business.

Then begin to focus on the beliefs attached to what you want

I could never do that I am not very intelligent

As soon as you begin to feel the emotional response state,

Let it go (your name) things will come right I am sure of it.

Most importantly when you say this really feel the relief of letting go, like that feeling when you have had a difficult day at work and you just flop down on a chair and allow your entire body to let go.

Then focus on the second belief

I would not know where to begin

Feel the emotional response

Let it go (your name) things will come right I am sure of it.

Feel the feeling of letting go

Focus on the third belief

I have lots of ideas but am scared things will not work out

Feel the emotional response

Let it go (your name), things will come right I am sure of it

Feel the feeling of letting go

And so on and so on with each belief feel the negative emotional response then use the words

Let it go (state your name); things will come right I am sure of it.

When you have gone through each of the beliefs concerning what you want to attract just bring yourself out of this relaxed state by counting up from 1 to 5. Now as you go through your day to day routine, should any of the old beliefs come back in, (and you will know by the emotional response you experience) just make the statement 'let it go (your name) things will come right I am sure of it: Feel the complete feeling of letting go. Do not be put off by the simplicity of this technique as it is extremely powerful when used correctly.

Summary

The reason this technique can work so effectively is because as we move through life we tend to argue against things that we do not want, see example below:-

What you want   **Belief**

I want a better job,   but I can't get it
I want to be well,   but I've never been well

I want more money,	but I cannot see how it will come
I want a good relationship,	but I am not very good looking
I want people to like me,	but they seem to take an instant dislike

It is very much like when two people are arguing the more they argue the more stubborn each person gets, the louder they get, and the firmer they get in their side of the argument (belief). If one person in the argument decided not to argue and just say "you are probably right, lets let it go now". What actually happens is no one persons beliefs have been compromised, in fact both persons have got what they want a harmonious relationship.

If you think of your emotional mind being very similar, you state what you want (thinking mind), then your beliefs (emotional mind), begin to list all the reasons why you cannot have it. When you make the decision to let go of the argument, you actually begin the process of attracting the very things that you want. The more you use this technique in your everyday life in all sorts of situations, the more you will begin to attract all the things that you want. It is best to only use this with one thing at a time at first. Eventually you will be able to use this technique when you want to attract lots of things in your life all at once.

Chapter 13
THE FANTASY TECHNIQUE

When to use the Technique

THIS TECHNIQUE IS QUITE A good technique for working with when you have a lot of beliefs. It is a useful technique in respect that it also allows you to create a positive emotional response to the things that you want to attract into your life, by using a singular word. Once this technique has been applied correctly you can then begin to use the singular word you have chosen to create the emotional response you want throughout the day. Therefore changing the old belief, allowing the law of attraction to bring to you whatever it is that you have asked for. This technique requires that you be in a relaxed state. It is good to use this technique if there are more than 5 beliefs regarding the subject of your attention (what you want to attract).

This technique is the only technique where you do not have to be aware of your current beliefs regarding what it is that you want to attract. You only have to be aware of the new beliefs that you want to create, regarding the things you want.

The example below is just an example but there is no reason why you could not use this technique to attract a new car, improved health in fact anything you wish. Just remember it works better when there are more than 5 beliefs surrounding the things that you want.

Example

Write on a piece of paper

What is it that I want to attract or experience?

I want to have a slim, slender body

Now, before you begin to utilise this technique I would like you to think of a trigger word or phrase that represents everything that you want to attract

In the example above you could use the word "slimmer"

If it were money you were trying to attract you could use the word 'Money' or 'successful'

The word you choose is of your choosing, as long as it relates to what you want to attract in your life.

To use this technique it is best to achieve a relaxed state of mind and body, using the relaxation technique described earlier.

Whilst in this relaxed state, I would like you to begin to create a fantasy of what you want to attract.

You could imagine yourself as you want to be: slim and slender. People around you are congratulating you on how fantastic you look. Notice how much more energy you have. How easy it is to eat what you want and feel so comfortable with this that you recognize when you have eaten enough and just make the decision to stop.

Or just enjoying wearing the new clothes that fit perfectly. The improved health.

Or even on holiday enjoying showing off your new slimmer physique on the beach. Enjoying swimming in the water and noticing others looking at your body in admiration of its wonderful size and shape.

Continue to do this until you can really feel the positive emotion flowing forth. When you feel this positive feeling flowing through you, continue with the rest of the technique. (remember your emotional mind does not know the difference between reality and imagination).

As you continue to do this your thoughts and emotions will continue to get stronger and stronger. When you feel they are at their peak, in other words when you feel really really good, begin to use the word, you have chosen to represent what you have asked for, so in this instance it would be the word 'slimmer'.

Begin to say the word slimmer inside yourself silently and mentally over and over saying the word "slimmer, slimmer, slimmer," continue to do this for about five or ten minutes whilst continuing to experience the wonderful fantasy of enjoying being slim.

After about five or ten minutes of this just count yourself up from 1 to 5 and bring yourself out of this calm peaceful state to a fully alert awakened state.

The next part to this exercise is:-

As you go through your day, just before you eat your meal, during your meal, after your meal; In fact anytime you like, use that key word' slimmer'.

Continue to state the key word inside yourself until you begin to feel the positive emotion flow. Once this happens you can stop.

Summary

What this technique actually achieves is what is called a positive anchor. For Example anytime you use the word 'slimmer' or whatever the word may be depending on what you have used the technique for, it allows positive emotion to flow forth. This in turn begins the process of creating the new belief system. This then allows the law of attraction to give you exactly what you have been asking for, which in this case is a slimmer slender body. Just for reference a positive anchor is a memory or associated experience where you have had a positive emotional response. An example of this would be a certain piece of music, or song you may hear that allows you to remember when you were doing something with someone that felt really good. Like a favourite song that a couple may share. This would be a positive anchor allowing the person to feel good when they hear the song. So what you are creating in the example above is a positive experience when you think of the word 'slimmer', allowing your emotional mind to re experience the fantasy you created within your mind, creating all the wonderful positive emotions for you. This technique should be used everyday until what you have asked for has manifested in your life. Use your key word as many times as you can during the day to allow the technique to work more quickly for you.

Chapter 14
THE FREEDOM TECHNIQUE

When to use the Technique

THIS TECHNIQUE IS A GOOD technique for working with when you have a lot of beliefs. This technique releases limiting beliefs, opening your mind up to the possibilities and potential of creating new beliefs. This in turn allows the law of attraction to bring to you the things that you want.

In the example below I am going to use this technique to attract a partner. I will show how the technique can be used and applied. I will first describe what is wanted, then the current beliefs surrounding it. I will then detail the new beliefs, and finally the application of the technique, to create the new beliefs, thereby attracting what you want into your experience.

If for any reason you are having difficulty identifying your current beliefs regarding what you want to attract, just think about what you do want and notice how you feel. If you feel a negative emotional response, then there are beliefs that are preventing you from attracting what you want, so begin to focus on those beliefs and list them.

The example below is just an example but there is no reason why you could not use this technique to attract a new car, improved health, in fact anything you wish. Just remember it works better when there are a lot of beliefs more than 5 surrounding the things that you want.

Example

Write on a piece of paper

What is it that I want to attract or experience?

I want to attract a loving partner who is compatible with me in every way.

What are my current beliefs regarding this?

I do not deserve to have a nice loving relationship.
There are no nice men / women, they are all the same.
It's so hard to find someone these days.
I feel so unhappy no one is in my life.
Who would want me?
I am too old to find anyone now.

There are probably many more that could be written above; however, I have just described a few of the possible beliefs that some people may have regarding relationships.

What new beliefs do I want to create regarding this condition?

I feel so good knowing that the law of attraction is bringing a partner to me right now. Someone who is compatible and in harmony with me in every single way.

Application of Technique

Now you have clarified your beliefs regarding what you want to attract you can begin applying the Freedom Technique. What I would like you to do first is to read the piece of paper you have so the current and new beliefs are fresh in your mind. The next step is to achieve a relaxed state of mind and body, using the relaxation technique described earlier.

Now whilst in this relaxed state of mind and body, I would like you to imagine you are in a room, very similar to a waiting room with lots of chairs and magazines and newspapers beside you. In front of you is one door leading out of the room, above this door is the word 'freedom'. Now as you look beside you, begin to notice the newspapers and magazines piled there. One newspaper in particular catches your eye. You notice the date, it is an old newspaper, and then you see a big picture of your self and below in typed print are the first of your beliefs:-

'I do not deserve to have a nice loving relationship'

Notice how it makes you feel to see it in black and white in that newspaper. Grab hold of the newspaper with both hands and begin to tear and rip the newspaper up into strips. As you do feel how good it is that you are getting rid of this old newspaper that is old news, not today's, then continue to throw the torn bits of newspaper into the bin beside you.

Now notice the newspaper that was underneath the first. Notice the date, it may be even older than the first newspaper, then you see another big picture of your self and below in typed print is the second of your beliefs:-

'There are no nice men and woman they are all the same'

Notice how it makes you feel to see it in black and white in that newspaper.
Grab hold of the newspaper with both your hands and begin to tear and rip the newspaper up into strips. As you do, feel how good it is that you are getting rid of this old newspaper that is old news, not today's, then continue to throw the torn bits of newspaper into the bin beside you.

Do this with each and every current belief that you have regarding the loving relationship you want to attract. Each has a newspaper notice the date, how old it is and how it makes you feel. Then with both hands tear and rip it into strips, feeling good that you are getting rid of it. Then throw it in the bin.

Once all the outdated old newspapers (beliefs) have been torn to shreds and thrown in the bin, you can then proceed with the next part of the technique.

If you look on the wall there is a unit that is called 'waste disposal unit'. I want you to empty the bin with all the old torn and shredded bits of newspaper down the disposal unit. They are not needed anymore, they are old news, so get rid of them down the shoot. Just feel how good it is to get rid of them.

Begin to notice the door at the other side of the room. The one called 'freedom'. Walk over to it notice its colour, its shape, its size, touch it, notice the temperature of the door. This door is very special as it is your door to freedom, freedom from outdated beliefs and thought patterns. Freedom to think, feel and believe what you want.

So as you reach for the handle to the door open it, and step over the threshold.   Feel how wonderful it is, light and airy, fresh and free. Notice there are windows instead of walls in this room, and every window is allowing the sunlight to shine into this room.   Notice the scenery through the windows;   there are oceans and beaches, forests and meadows, in fact all sorts of wonderful things.

This room just feels so free.

Notice in the centre of the room there is one solitary newspaper.

Notice there is a large picture of you, with your partner (the money, health and so on, that you want to attract), and you can see yourself smiling.

As you read the large headlines above the picture notice that the headlines are similar to your new belief, except the newspaper states that you have that partner right now.

'I feel so good knowing that the law of attraction has brought a partner to me right now.   Someone who is compatible and in harmony with me in every single way'.

As you look at the date of the newspaper you see why, this is your future, the one you are now moving towards, the one the law of attraction is bringing to you.   Begin to notice the excited feeling, the feeling of positive expectation moving through your body.   As you begin to feel confident in the knowledge that what you have asked to come to you is now on its way.   The newspaper from the future is confirmation of that.

Then when you are ready count yourself up from 1 to five returning to a normal waking alert state.

This exercise should be continued on a daily basis until what you have asked for has manifested in your life. You may find that as you return to that waiting room there may be more newspapers (beliefs) to get rid of or none at all. Everyone is individual so everyone's experience will be different. But faithfully applied this technique will bring you what you want.

Summary

What this exercise is extremely good at doing is communicating to your emotional mind, in a very symbolic way, (which is actually how the emotional mind communicates), that you no longer want certain beliefs and patterns of thought. It also creates a feeling of belief and positive expectation within you that what you have asked for is on its way. When you obtain that good feeling about what you want to attract, and also have that positive expectation that you are moving towards the things that you want to attract. That is when the law of attraction begins to bring those situations, people, things and experiences to you.

Chapter 15

THE PROBLEM SOLVING TECHNIQUE

When to use this Technique

THIS TECHNIQUE IS A GOOD technique when you are not sure what to do, or need an answer about a certain situation or problem you are experiencing.

It is also good to use when you lack clarity, or experience confusion. This technique does not require you to be aware of any specific beliefs. All that is required for this technique to work, is an openness of mind, to trust that you mind has the power to attract all solutions and answers to you. If you have already used some of the techniques in this book, then you will already have a certain amount of belief and trust in the power of your mind, to attract to you whatever it is you want. Your emotional mind has great wisdom and knowledge. Where this knowledge is unavailable to your emotional mind; it has the capability by using the powerful law of attraction, to attract the solution or answers to whatever it is that you want to know.

Example

Write on a piece of paper

What is it the solution or answer I am seeking

In this example we will use the example of

I want my own business, but I have no idea what to do.

Application of Technique

The next step is to achieve a relaxed state of mind and body, using the relaxation technique described earlier.

Whilst in this relaxed state of mind and body, just for a few minutes begin to ponder, and think about the solution, answer to the problem you are seeking.

What I would like you to do is imagine just how powerful your mind is. It contains all the knowledge of your experiences of life. It retains all the things you have learned and understood. There have probably been many times in your life where you have had good ideas, no matter how simple or complicated they may be. an example of a few are below:-

If I go down this street it will be quicker.
If I place items in this cupboard it will be easier to reach them.
If I take this job it will be more money
If I carry out that particular action it will work

Just the simple statements above, are examples of ideas you may have had. You wanted to find a better, quicker, more beneficial way of doing something, your mind assimilated all data and came up with a solution. So in many ways your mind is continually giving you new ideas.

I would like you to imagine yourself in a safe private place, somewhere that is secure and peaceful. It could be a private, beach, a room in your house, a beautiful scene from nature, or it could even be just a space inside your own mind. Once you have done this know that this place is secure and private: Your place. Begin to focus on contacting your emotional mind, just ponder and think about what it would be like. Imagine how that part of you would look. Would it be a colour, a shape, an image of some person or animal? Or would it be a feeling or voice, or just a knowing that it is there. It does not matter, your experience is unique. Begin to invite that part of yourself into this private space you have created. Some people speak of a calm peaceful feeling flowing through their bodies it can be like a feeling of meeting an old friend you have not seen in a long while.

Now begin to talk to your emotional self about the problem, or question that you want to know the answer to. It can be anything, on absolutely any subject of your choosing.

Once you have asked what you want to ask, being as detailed as you can, just sit in silence for a few moments, and imagine how you would feel if you had the answer now. How would you be standing, what thoughts would you have, what would you be feeling, how would you be living your life. Sometimes the answer to whatever you have asked can be given to you right now in this moment. However, in most instances, the answer may come to you later on in the day, or a few days later. The most important thing about this technique is not to feel effort. Just turn the problem over to your emotional mind, wait a few minutes, experiencing what it would be like if you had the solution, answer right now then bring yourself out of this relaxed state by counting up from 1 to 5, to a fully alert awakened state.

As you go through your daily life, should the problem, question arise during the day, just say to yourself in a carefree way 'I know the answer is coming' and carry on with your day. If you have received no answer, or possible solution, or idea, within 30 days of making your request carry out the exercise again. However usually the answers flow forth during the same day or just a few days later.

Summary

This technique is different from the rest as there are no beliefs attached to what you want. All you are doing is turning over the problem, question to your emotional mind. This technique only needs to be used once for each situation unless the answer, solution you have been asking for has not been answered within 30 days, then you can carry out the technique again.

I have used this technique many times when I have lost something and cannot remember where I have put it. I just ask for assistance in finding what I have lost, and usually within 24hrs I find it. My friends actually call me 'the finder of lost objects', because I seem to be so good at finding items they have lost too, by carrying out the same technique.

Chapter 16

THE AFFIRMATION
TECHNIQUE

When to use the Technique

I HAVE LEFT THIS TECHNIQUE until last as this technique can also assist you in situations when you are in conversations with people who hold and speak their negative beliefs to you or even direct them at you. As described in previous chapters language is extremely powerful and can affect your emotions. Your emotional response to the words spoken then emits signals from you, changing your point of attraction. This can delay or even prevent the law of attraction from bringing all the things you have been asking for, into your experience. Being able to divert your attention elsewhere when you are bombarded with negative conversations from those around you, can allow you to continue to emit positive signals. This in turn allows the law of attraction to continue working for you, bringing all that you have asked for into your experience quickly and effortlessly.

This technique is extremely good if you like directness and want to be very specific and direct to your emotional mind. The direct approach can change certain beliefs and thought patterns you may hold, that are preventing you from receiving whatever you want to attract. To explain this technique fully I will describe two situations where it can be used as detailed below:-

The first technique will describe affirmations and what they are and how to implant them firmly in your emotional mind.

The second technique describes how affirmations can be used, throughout your day. For example, when you are in situations with friends, family, colleagues in fact anyone you know, where the conversation is quite negative, creating a negative feeling within you.

Once you begin to apply this technique into your life, in a very short time indeed you will begin to notice the benefit. You may find that you will be free from the effect that other peoples negative words and actions have upon you. Instead, you will have complete freedom to think and feel exactly what you want, which will be focusing on the things you want the law of attraction to bring to you. You will already be in a positive attraction state so it will be so much easier for you to get the things that you want.

Affirmations

What is an affirmation?

There are many descriptions of what an affirmation is. My interpretation of an affirmation is:-

'A firm positive and direct statement that bridges two beliefs'

What I actually mean by this, is if someone is overweight and they use the affirmation 'I am slim' or 'I am getting slimmer' the emotional mind will reject it instantly. The reason for this is that when you look in the mirror you see you are not slim and no steps have been taken to change that.

An affirmation that would bridge that belief would be

"I recognise that I am overweight right now, however each day I will begin to notice changes in the way that I eat and move my body, allowing me to reduce the fat around my body".

Notice how effortless the above statement feels as you read it. The reason for this is that there is no contradiction of beliefs between the thinking and emotional minds. Basically you have created a bridge that is believable to your emotional mind, of where you are and where you want to be.

How to create affirmations

Once you understand the principles about creating an affirmation then it is quite simple to create them to fit any circumstance or situation.

The first thing about an affirmation is to identify where you are, so if we continue but this time use another example, lets say someone wants to attract more money into their experience, but are suffering great poverty at the moment.

So if we identify where you are.

'I am always in debt and have no money'

That is the current belief

Now we would want to bridge this to the new belief.

So using the example above we could say:-

1 *'I am always in debt and have no money, but as I move through life, I am becoming more open and aware of opportunities around me that can allow money to come into my life'.*

2 *'I am always in debt and have no money, but I am becoming richer and richer with each day'.*

Notice the two example above they may seem like a simple playing with words. What I would like you to notice is the feeling between the two affirmations above. The first affirmation is working within your belief system so it feels effortless and believable. The second affirmation is not believable to your emotional mind, as nothing has happened yet. This can then begin to create a negative attraction.

What I would like you to understand is that the first affirmation is a bridge from where you are to where you want to be, in other words, it is believable to the emotional mind, there is no contradiction. This then allows the law of attraction to set things in motion to attract what you want.

The second affirmation is implying that things have started to change, which they have not of course. This instantly creates a feeling of not having what you have asked for which then creates a negative feeling (Contradiction) within you preventing the law of attraction from bringing what you want.

This is the reason that so many people can not get affirmations to work effectively. One of the first things I talk to clients about when they come to see me is the use of language. The reason being it is so powerful, and affects all of us in so many ways.

I will now detail how you can create your affirmation and give a couple of examples. There are three steps to creating an affirmation:

1   Identify where you are, situation you are in
2   Create a bridge to where you want to go
3   Positive firm affirmations of what you want.

Let me show you how this works in the table below

Where you are	Bridge	Positive Firm Affirmation of what you want
I always seem to be ill.	Everyday I am	Noticing an improvement in my condition
I am always in debt and never seem to have enough money.	As I move through life I am becoming more open and aware	Of opportunities around me to let more money come into my life.
I tried so many things to lose weight and nothing works.	If I learn to trust in my body	My eating habits could begin to change allowing me to become the size and shape I choose.
I never seem to get on in work.	Each and every day I can begin to notice around me	more and more opportunities to succeed in my career.
I have tried so hard to stop smoking.	Each day it is becoming easier and easier	To picture myself as a non smoker, free, healthy and happy.
Its so hard to run a successful prosperous business.	I have a fantastic mind, that produces wonderful ideas	One of those ideas could allow my business to flourish and prosper.

If you notice the affirmation implies how easy and effortless things can come to you. It is just a change of words, however, that simple change of words can determine whether you are attracting negatively or positively.

When creating your own affirmations it is a good idea to use a table as above, that way you can instantly notice how you feel as you read the affirmation. A good feeling as you read the affirmation will let you know that it will work for you attracting what you want.

Now you have your affirmation we want to use it.

Example

Write your affirmation on a piece of paper.

In this example we will use one from the table above

'As I move through life I am becoming more open and aware of opportunities around me to let more money come into my life'

Application of Technique

Technique 1

The next step is to achieve a relaxed state of mind and body, using the relaxation technique described earlier.

The technique for implanting an affirmation into your mind is really simple. Once you have achieved the relaxed state of mind and body just begin to state your affirmation in a relaxed care free way, like a lullaby. This requires no effort, any effort on your part actually hinders the process, just allow the affirmation to be in a completely natural carefree way.

Think of it like this if you were asking someone to help you to do something in particular, perhaps help you with the shopping or in the garden, you would not boss them about. You would ask them in a casual positive way, so that person would actually want to help you. This is the same process for implanting your affirmation. As you have created an affirmation that bridges two beliefs, there are no contradictions. All you want is your emotional mind to help you accept the affirmation and begin to attract to you what you want. So the easiest way is in a casual carefree way.

Take your time to implant the affirmation repeating the affirmation as many times as you wish. As you do this you can usually feel as though the affirmation has been accepted, or just a feeling of peace. That is ok, when you achieve this you can just count yourself out of this relaxed state by counting up from 1 to 5.

You can carry out this exercise just the once, or every single day, it is entirely up to you. What I would suggest is that you keep the piece of paper with the affirmation written on it and throughout your day read it many times creating that calm comfortable feeling. Before long you will begin to notice that you really do feel that feeling of belief within you as you are reading the affirmation. When this happens the attraction process has started, and it will not be too long before what you have asked for has manifested in your life.

Technique 2

This technique works by allowing you an understanding that at any one time you are the person who controls and decides what you feel.

Let's give you a few examples

1.) Whilst driving you car someone pulls out in front of you.

Did you feel anger? Were you angry with your passengers? Did your blood pressure increase? Did adrenalin get released into your body? Just look at what has happened as a result of a total STRANGER pulling out in front of you.

2.) You are at work, and your boss says you have not done that right; you always seem to do things incorrectly.

How do you feel? Do your emotions take a turn for the worst? Do you criticise yourself? Do you get angry? Do you get really upset? Do you take these worries home with you at night to your family and friends?

3.) You are with your partner who is not understanding your point of view. Do you feel angry, hurt she / he does not understand? Frustrated you cannot get your viewpoint across?

Who created those feelings? Was it the surroundings? The people you were with?, **WHO?**

Well, I am here to tell you that there is only one person who can control how you feel, and that is **YOU.** Only you can think your thoughts, and only you can feel what you feel. If you have experienced any of those situations above, or others where you have experienced similar emotional responses, then you basically have allowed those other persons or situations to control you, and the way you feel. Very much like a Puppet on a string is controlled by the puppet master. Only in this instance you are the puppet on a string, and the situation or person that is causing you to respond negatively is the puppet master.

There is a really good technique that if applied and used consistently can change the way you feel under any circumstance or situation whether it is your partner, boss or whoever is screaming at you, you can still remain in a good emotional place, thereby continuing to attract what you want. The wonderful thing about this, is once it becomes dominant within you, those things that caused you to feel negative will be gone. The situation will change and become more positive, as you will be attracting more positive experiences, conversations and situations.

For this technique to be successful it is good to memorise your affirmation so that you can use it anywhere under any circumstances.

I use the affirmation below, you can too if you choose. If you do choose to create one of your own it needs to be generic enough to fit any and all situations where you may feel a negative emotion.

'Even though this is happening to me right now, I know that my feelings are mine and I choose to feel good right now. As I feel good I begin to attract more and more positive conversations and situations into my life'

It is a good idea to begin using this affirmation for two weeks before applying it in your own life situations. To do this just follow the same process as technique 1.

Now you have implanted this affirmation firmly into your emotional mind, any time you are in a situation that is creating a negative emotional response within you, just say to yourself **STOP**, *then begin to repeat silently and mentally the affirmation you have created.*

At first you may need to do this several times or more in various situations before you begin to really notice a difference in the way that you feel. If you continue to use this technique, in as little as 30 days you can begin to notice how different you feel in many different situations with all sorts of people. When this happens those situations and people that created the negative feelings within you, will either go out of your life, or you will begin to notice that when you are with them, you only see the best of them.

Summary

The techniques outlined above are extremely good for bridging belief systems from where you are now to where you want to be. The wonderful thing about this technique is that it allows you to feel good under almost any circumstance. Once you have achieved this, everything you have ever wanted, or dreamed of, can come to you so much more quickly. The reason for this is that you will be in a positive attraction state most of the time which then allows the law of attraction to respond to you in a positive way bringing everything that you want.

Chapter 17
MORE ABOUT USING THE TECHNIQUES

ANY OF THE TECHNIQUES DESCRIBED earlier can be used together or in isolation. The only thing I would say is that when first utilising one or two techniques together it is a good idea to work on one subject at a time. So if you want to attract more money you could use:

The agreement technique at first to allow the emotional mind to agree with your intent. The next day you could then utilise the movie strip or genie technique to begin the process of attracting what you want. The affirmation technique could then be used in situations where you experience a negative emotional response.

The key thing to remember about mixing techniques is that it needs to feel comfortable to you. If you choose not to mix the techniques it is still ok to just use one technique at a time.

The mixing of techniques does not increase the effectiveness, it just allows you the variety and creativity to play about with them using them as and when they suit your individual needs:

The thing to know is that all the techniques are extremely powerful on their own and if you only ever use one technique from this book, it can still create that positive attraction. This allows the law of attraction to bring everything into your life that you want.

All of the techniques described in this book have been created to allow you to change your current belief systems so that you can then begin to get what you want in life. How you choose to use these techniques is entirely up to you.

For me personally the techniques are so incorporated into my life that it just seems like the most natural thing in the world to me. It allows me to have a wonderful, happy and prosperous life, as it will for you too.

The other thing to note is that as you use the techniques you will find that you become quicker at creating changes in your belief systems. The reason being is that your emotional mind will create new habits to facilitate these quicker changes in your belief systems. In effect, you emotional mind will expect you to change certain beliefs.

Remember beliefs are not written in stone, and if you apply the techniques in this book, whether by mixing one, two or three, of them. YOU CAN change those beliefs that have prevented you from getting what you want.

Part Three
CONCLUSION

Chapter 18
QUESTIONS AND ANSWERS

IN MY EXPERIENCE AS A hypnotherapist, I have been asked many questions regarding the principles and techniques outlined in this book. Below I have compiled a list of the most commonly asked questions, with possible answers and solutions.

What is the reason that bigger things seem harder to attract that the little things?

The answer to this question lies in your beliefs. If you believe something is extremely big and will take a long time to come then it will. The techniques in this book will assist you in changing those beliefs. If you ask for something whether it be a million pounds, or just one hundred pounds it can come to you. All you have to do is have that complete confidence, faith and trust that whatever it is you have asked for is on its way to you. That is all that is required (positive expectation).

How long will it take before I see results?

This is not an easy question to answer as everyone is different, and everyone has different belief systems. If you begin by attracting small things first, which will manifest quicker because there will be no, or fewer beliefs surrounding them. This will allow your confidence to grow using the techniques. Eventually you will be able to manifest anything you want as quickly as you expect the things that you want to come. A lot of people begin to notice evidence of what they want coming into their lives within 30 days of beginning the techniques.

How do I know I am doing the technique right?

There is no right or wrong way to perform the techniques everyone is unique with unique experiences. All that is required for the techniques to work, is to approach them with an open mind and carefree attitude and your emotional mind will accept the changes you want to make, attracting to you whatever it is that you have asked for.

What happens if the affirmation is not correctly worded?

If an affirmation is not worded correctly you will know by the way it feels. A good rule of thumb is, if it feels like hard work or uncomfortable in anyway as you read the affirmation do not use it and create another. An affirmation should feel comfortable, and effortless. If for any reason you cannot think of an affirmation that can create the effect you want. You can use any out of this book or use the Fantasy Technique to create a singular word that you can use with the Affirmation Technique.

Can I attract anything?

Yes you can, as long as you believe you can. That is the key word belief. If you are asking for the perfect relationship but do not believe that you really deserve it then you will not attract it. The techniques in this book can help you to change old outdated beliefs. If the techniques are followed faithfully, there is no reason whatsoever that you could not attract anything you want into your life.

Can I use this to feel better about me, to increase my confidence and self esteem?

Yes you can, and I would actively encourage this as the way that you feel determines your point of attraction. Good techniques to use for this are the Agreement Technique and the Gratitude Technique.

Can I use this to attract a particular person into my life?

No, as we all create our own reality, your intentions may conflict with the specific person you are trying to attract. The best way is to ask for someone who is right and perfect for you right now.

What would be a good way to mix the techniques?

I will give an example below:

Lets say you wanted to own a successful business.

You could use the Agreement Technique first to allow your emotional mind to be aware and agree with your intentions.

If you did not know what type of business you would like you could then use the Problem Solving Technique.

To finish off you could then use the Gratitude Technique, so it then allows your emotional mind to get into the feeling place of what you want.

Once a week carry on with the Agreement Technique acknowledging how wonderful your emotional mind is working for you and throughout the days after continue to use the Gratitude Technique.

There is no rule that says you should mix these techniques in any specific way. Use whatever techniques feel comfortable for you. Play with the techniques, you cannot get it wrong, see what works best for you.

The thing is I am really depressed right now how can I attract a way to feel better.

A really good technique for this is the Letting Go Technique. I use this a lot with clients who are suffering from depression or anxiety. It is a wonderful effortless way of letting go of those emotions and beliefs that are no longer appropriate. If used over a period of 30 days consistently and faithfully a gradual improvement should be noticed which will then allow you to use one of the other techniques such as the Genie Technique.

If language affects my point of attraction, what about when I watch the news or read a newspaper about something awful or bad that is happening, can this change my point of attraction?

Yes, anything that creates an emotion within you changes your point of attraction. The best thing is not to watch or read newspapers. Should you choose to, you could use something like the Gratitude Technique after reading that newspaper or after watching that TV programme and use an affirmation should as:-

'Thank you so much for all the good things that are in my life, and that I am free from the emotional responses of those newspapers and TV programmes'

You could also use the affirmation technique too. When you are reading those newspapers or watching that TV programme, you could use the affirmation several times during the experience to allow your emotional response to change. The important thing to remember, is that the more you begin to feel positive emotion, the less of those things will be attracted to you or into your experience.

How can I get to the tipping point quicker?

By using the techniques more frequently you can achieve the tipping point where the new belief becomes stronger than the old belief.

What If I am sceptical and do not really believe these techniques will work?

Many of the people I have seen in my career as a hypnotherapist arrive on my doorstep sceptical. All that is required for the techniques to work is that you really want what you want to attract and are willing to just allow yourself the opportunity to have a go anyway. If you approach the techniques with a carefree attitude such as, 'Well, I have got nothing to lose whether it works or not, so I will just give it a go' If you adopt this attitude and start off with small things at first you will be amazed at the results. As your belief in the techniques becomes stronger the scepticism will diminish.

Can I manifest more than one thing at a time?

Yes, you can manifest as many things as you choose. It is good at first to just manifest one thing at a time, until you get used to using the techniques. What you will also find is that as you focus on just attracting one experience, situation, thing at a time, the results will come much faster.

I have tried so hard to apply the techniques but nothing has happened.

Within the question lies the problem, that word 'try' it implies effort and will power. These techniques do not require effort or willpower, they are meant as a way to actually allow your thought processes (beliefs) to be adjusted. Your mind does all of this, all you are doing is implanting the idea of what you want. The law of attraction then responds to the new ideas you have implanted within your emotional mind.

I would say use the techniques again, however this time adopt a casual attitude about it similar to when you are on holiday lying on the beach daydreaming. If you adopt a casual relaxed way about it, and just daydream the technique, it will be so much more effective for you in bringing all that you have asked for.

I do not want to work for money, is there a way that I can attract money by winning it?

Yes you can. However, I always teach people to focus on the outcome rather than the how? The thing is that if you focus on the outcome, for example already having the money, the law of attraction has many avenues and ways it can bring the money to you in a way that is effortless, fun and comfortable for you. When you focus on the how (winning the money), unless you are in the place of real belief that you will get it, it will not be attracted, which can then create doubts within you and hinder the whole process of you creating your own reality, the reality that you want.

I am already in a relationship, and am deeply in love with my partner, but my partner seems to criticise me all the time. How do I make our relationship better?

The answer to this question is to change your point of attraction. Remember your life is like a huge gigantic mirror reflecting everything back at you. So for example if you do not feel very secure in yourself, the relationship, or even doubt that you deserve this relationship, this will be reflected back at you in the criticism you are receiving. I would apply the movie strip technique for this so it can allow you to change your beliefs regarding relationships, including the relationship with yourself. Then you could apply the Gratitude Technique, this can then allow you to emit new signals which the law of attraction can then respond to, bringing the improved relationship to you.

What is the best way to deal with difficult people?

The Affirmation Technique is really effective at allowing you to react differently, and most importantly feel differently, when you are with difficult people. Once you begin using this technique in the way described it will change your point of attraction and those difficult people will either move out of your life or react differently around you.

I am not very good at visualising, will it still work?

Yes it will, If I were to ask you now what colour is your car, or your front door, or even what number is recorded on your front door. Most people would be able to do that. That is the degree of visualisation, imagination that is required for the techniques to work. The most important thing with these techniques is not the images, but the feelings that are evoked within you as you use the techniques.

I am not feeling anything, am I doing something wrong? Will it still work?

Usually when this happens it can be caused by a number of things. It could be that you have not achieved a deep enough state of relaxation, or that you are meeting resistance to the changes from your emotional mind.

A good way of dealing with this is to achieve the relaxed state of mind, then apply the Agreement Technique to allow your emotional mind to be aware of what it is that you want to do, and most importantly agree to it.

If you still feel nothing after this you could actually achieve the relaxed state and then think of the most wonderful memory that you have, it can be anything:

A holiday somewhere.
Your back garden.
A feeling of pride when you passed your driving test.
A birthday or wedding.
In fact any special moment that created a positive emotion within you.

Now begin to experience that moment as though you are actually there re-living it. Take your time, allow the memory to come in its own natural way. As you continue to do this for five or ten minutes you will begin to notice a positive emotion beginning to flow through you from the experience. Then it is at this point you can begin to use the technique. After this you will find it much easier next time to apply the technique.

(Remember your emotional mind does not know the difference between reality and imagination, so once you create a powerful

enough memory, you can begin to experience the associated positive feelings attached to that memory).

What is the best technique for attracting lots of money?

Any of the techniques are good for this, in fact you can use any of the techniques and apply them into any area of your life. The only thing that is important is that you feel comfortable about using the particular technique you have chosen.

Chapter 19
FINAL WORDS

Now we have come to the end of this book, and I just know that this book is going to be just as enjoyable for you reading it, as it has been for me writing it.

As my life continues to flow wonderfully and harmoniously from one experience to another, in perfect synchronicity with all the things that I want and dream of. I now know that I have also given you all the tools you need so that you can begin the process of achieving your dreams too.

This book is a beginners guide, a guide to living life to the full, utilising the potential of your own mind to let the law of attraction bring everything to you. I feel excited about all of you reading this book and applying the techniques in your own lives to attract everything that you want, and as you gain experience in using the techniques and applying them in your own lives, you will begin to feel a wonderful exhilaration for life. As you gradually come to the realisation that everything, absolutely everything in your life is under your control, the experiences you have, the people you meet, the money you have, the relationships you are in, or in the process of attracting, the improved health, in fact all of it, is created by you as a result of the thoughts beliefs and emotions that you experience in your life.

In future books I will include more about the law of attraction and advanced techniques for you, to utilise in specific areas of your life, such as relationships, money, health and so on. However, for know I wish you happy dreaming and manifesting. Remember nothing is to big to attract, so think, dream, manifest and enjoy life.

www.freedomhypnosis.org.uk

Printed in the United Kingdom by
Lightning Source UK Ltd., Milton Keynes
141304UK00002B/4/P